PERFECT. SCAR

Robert Chevara

Published April 2022 by
Team Angelica Publishing,
an imprint of Angelica Entertainments Ltd

Team Angelica Publishing
51 Coningham Road
London W12 8BS

www.teamangelica.com

A CIP catalogue record for this book is available from the British
Library

ISBN 978-1-9163561-9-1

*(A note on the fonts used in this book: the text is predominantly
Mongolian Baiti; the title Edo; 'I see all my friends' and 'Flowers
that bloom tomorrow' Zenaida.)*

To Miss Patricia Killaspy, my aunt.

With love and admiration.

'If I got rid of my demons, I'd lose my angels.'

Tennessee Williams

Foreword
by Rikki Beadle-Blair

Robert was always a poet. Back when we were 15-year-old South-East London kids meeting up at the Old Vic Youth Theatre, he carried out-of-date diaries around with him re-purposed as notebooks, every page covered with his beautiful calligraphic handwriting. Everyone he met he'd ask, 'Would you like to hear my new poem?' before, without waiting for an answer, standing up and reading it aloud in a deep resonant voice. Everywhere we hung out in those days, the foyer of the National Theatre, the cafés in the National Film Theatre (now the BFI) and the Royal Festival Hall, Robert would read. On buses home to the Old Kent Road, or tubes into the West End and Notting Hill, as our orbit widened, Robert was constantly writing and reading. How did he see so much while so often looking down? He acted back then. Then he became a director, then a theatre and opera director, then a librettist and translator. Always expanding. And Robert is great at all of it. Intelligent. Passionate. Uncompromising. Unlimited. But Robert has always been a poet. He wrote poems into the fly-leaves of books, or on the title page of book gifts. He wrote poems to celebrate and poems to commiserate. That summer we spent in Athens when we were eighteen, he wrote a ton of poetry. Recently in the Pandemic I found an arty scrapbook (scrappy art-book?) I'd made out of photos we'd taken that summer to illustrate poems by Robert. Or was it the other way round?

I don't remember creating the book. Just that I took a lot of photos and that Robert wrote a lot of poems. His Byronic hair, his expressive delicate but strong hands, his piercing but soft blue eyes, his incisive wit, boundless vocabulary, supernatural sixth sense, breathtaking intelligence and his soulful voice. Robert was a poem. The total romantic. The sensual buccaneer.

The diva with soaring vocals. (Oh, he sings too! Like a South London Mahalia Jackson, honey.) A poet and a poem.

When we met, punk was the thing and disco was hated by everyone except the gays. We loved both. Our curiosity was boundless. Music, Film, Books, Theatre, Dance, Politics, we loved it all. And Robert taught me soooo much.

We haven't changed. Still travelling, still creating, still exploring, still mad fans of everything. Every week there are emails and texts. Have you seen this? Read this? Heard about this? We are still fifteen, you know, a pair of high-art to low-culture fanboys, still curious, still finding our way in the world, my brother and I. And now finally he's publishing his poems. I thought: he's forgotten about that part of him. I was wrong. Here's a new bunch of 'em, 45 years after the day I first heard one. And I'm proud to be the one to introduce you to them.

Have you met my brother Robert Chevara? He's a poet you know. He's a poem.

Rikki

Contents

The Dancer Upstairs

Rapture. Deliberate, fleeting.
So subtle. So apt.
Euphoria engulfing, thrilling, delicate and
terrifying.
Difficult to capture.

Crack Crack Whack
on the wooden floor.
Mean. Foul.
Hard to fathom why it's erotic.
The outbreath as he lifts, twists his partner –
it's barely there, but tangible.

Quixotic.

That smell of ambition, hunger, greed –
an aroma like no other.

Giselle.

Joy. So different to happiness. Ecstatic and singular.
Every dancer knows that.

Running in the sunlight. Secrets
with friends. That

unuttered, that wordless wish.
Hushed and hovering,
barely there. But radiating.
Eating the air.

But then, what did he say?

'Nothing good gets away.
 Nothing good gets away.'

I hear you

There was no way, no mere breakthrough
when getting close to you.
My hold, your life
and the exchange we drew
with my blood and your
spit, my breath, your
shit.

How close, how close,
how close we are.
The icy look, the perfect scar.
The mirror image: me and you,
kissing and cursing,
submerging, subsuming,
we breathe the breath.

Encircling. Grounding, those memories,
both voluntary and unwilling.

But when I'm alone, I clearly see, how far
you are from me.

The living space,
the silent empty air,
full of danger and charm.
And thirst.

We.

Laden with meaning,
exhausted by exposition,
in amber, in aspic,
yet even while frozen, floating,
touching but not breaking the surface...

In your eyes mountains and valleys flecked with red.
Defiant, dazzling,
a volcano,
a furnace,
insatiable hunger.

A singular reflection.

Room

How did we get there?
That box
so bloody, black and bare.

The rancid air
inside that room
the guilt and pleasure
envelops, imprisons, seduces us.

Etched in acid
we are forever caught,
forever there.
Spied through the dust,
us.

After a day not eating
lying next to each other. So still.
After two days straight,
we hallucinate.

The walls are transparent
and people are looking in,
pressing their faces to the glass.
All we ask is quiet
and solitude.
And the tears, endless
in this pale green fishbowl.

Cleaving to each other as if drowning.
The caress. The pietà.
(Is that going too far?)

We tumbled and
wrestled. Fell endlessly
into an eternal void.
Only we. Trapped in that room,
could see
how far we'd fallen.

In the voice of a lisping child I said,
'I love you, Mother, don't go.'
Endlessly laughing, endlessly singing,
electricity cracking, joyous and free,
you'd already escaped me.

Straight into the sunlit night.

MAN. I. FEST. O

I am not a homosexual
I'm a HOMO
I'm not a homosexual.
I'm a HOMO.
And renegade.
And serious.
And retrograde.
Delirious.

I'm more Genet than Gide.
Agreed.
I'm more Genet than Proust.
There's proof.

I'm predatory.
Greedy. Needy.
Not made for comfort and calm.
I'll harm.

Not good gay. Bad?
Can labelling send you mad?
My sex – thought,
not bought,
but earned.
Right here. It's right there for all to see,
I'm not lovable.
I'm fuckable.
Handgrenade, me.

Arseholes? Yes please.
Obsession and hunger.
Desire the liar.

I am drugs, said Dali,
but he hadn't met me.
I'd have fucked him hard and long
if we'd met.
Brando. Franco.
Arse in the air Channing Tatum.
Sal Mineo.

The personal as political.
Yes, indeed.
The physical political.

As in all art,
the good should tear us apart.

Insomnia

To dive into that black gloss, that velvet,
that hole.
Or is it indigo?
I swim and swim
trying to breathe
evenly,
trying not to panic.
Don't let the fear in.

I'm afraid to lie in that huge bed.

It's a pool I can't
climb out from.
Where the dead float
and beckon
with reassuring smiles.

Come, they say.
Be.

Room 2

Turn the key.
Slowly.
Click. Click. Click.
Now we are free.

You you
you, go first.

Graceful, light and golden –
dreamed yourself there, dreamed yourself up
beautifully
for all to see

insomnia, your friend
who wedded me
whispered alluringly
in the night.
Sometimes, in broad daylight,
bedded me.

I heard. I saw
Si Si Si

A lover bereft,
left.

I'd see us, we'd float on a magic carpet.
So high. So high

yet not quite hitting the azure
nor reaching the sky.

Icarus and Medea,
Alice and Tommy,
Normal Norman,
Mother Lü.*
Me and you.

These roles we give ourselves.
These lies we feed ourselves
and each other.

Hear me, mother.

(* Alice and Tommy are mother and son in *Alice Doesn't Live Here Anymore*. Normal Norman is Norman Bates in *Psycho*. Mother Lü started a peasant uprising in China in 18 CE, after her son was executed by the government for a minor offence. She captured the supervisor who ordered his death. The county officials begged for mercy for him, but she reminded them that her son had received no mercy and had his head chopped off. She was the first female rebel leader in Chinese history.)

The Radiates

Cold. Cold.
Grey cold, black cold.
Dark, damp earth.
Mould.

The old believers and the true,
Penda's men, raw valleys and steel.
Resurrection, anew.
Penda's fen. More
Celtic than Saxon,
more pagan than plainsong.

Inanimate. Eternal. Burning.

Forever a labyrinth. Secret. Obscene.

Those whispers still echo,
through
madness, mud. Green.

Ancient and anarchic
dreamlike and cathartic

gloaming fields
still throb
with meaning and misuse.

Those ancient ways do not die so easily,
but slumber. And murmur
in the ash tree's leaves.

'We are still what we were before. Before.
Come, or we'll return. Each
tree is a door. Each
ancient road, each crossroads, leads to us.
A pathway and an altar.

Breathe deeply and we're there,
rustling in your hair.'

Violet Creams

Ivory. Oh ivory
and pale green eyes.
Red, red and freckles.
Freckles. Hated.
Freckled and speckled and beautiful.

Silk scarves covering crimson hair.
So shameful and ashamed.

A lifetime of working for men
less intelligent, less able than you
would damage and demean
self-esteem. Erode
that delicate sense of worth.

All were answered with calm kindness, reserve and bite.

Helping, holding.

Helping,
from that deep well of understanding, resignation and pain.

And disdain
for anything that was crude, that lacked
empathy.

Was it a problem

there was never a me in your me?

Honourably, clearly,

'I'm invisible,' you'd say, 'and I prefer it that way.'

Reticent, withheld
so you could watch,
teach, watch, help,
watch, critique. Watch.

Those long period pains were hard and heavy,
locked in your room.
'For what?' you'd say. 'For what!?'

'I loved once, but I was too afraid
couldn't invite him in.'

A decision was made.
Never again to experience that pain,
but remain
at one remove.

Remote. Alive.

Private Painful Passionate.

Eyesight failing, heart attacks,
stealing, smoking,
dignity intact.

A life of men cut out of family photos.

And dreams.
And violet creams.

I SEE ALL MY FRIENDS

i see all my friends now
look at the boys and girls.
eyes follow hungrily. fascinated. follow their
gaze to broad backs, narrow hips
great skin. refreshed, moist. manner
confident and easy.
this is no longer us.
we are not easy.

i never wear shoes
anymore. proper shoes. when i do i look like divine
strutting in downtown baltimore.
or sophia loren in it happened in naples.

or this is what i think i look like...

and it happened. it did happen

many times.
many times. i was seen. and now when
strangers look at us? there's what? a curiosity?
no hunger, nothing
insatiable, but maybe there's an interest
a door slightly ajar,
to peep through
at who we were.
what we carried.

what we knew.
but those young, young, young, young men and
women,
laughing, intimate, intricate, striding
don't acknowledge our stare.
or even let us know they know it's there.

THE TEXTURES OF THE SANE

The textures of the sane –
I have tried to grasp them.

Signals, smiles, looks, disdain.
I interpret with a fathomless gaze

So close. I feel the heat of their breath,
singeing me.

As if standing at the bedside of a dying man I
can't catch his last whisper.

I mouth his mumble back at him,
but have not really heard.

SYLVIA

There's still no-one like you
who could do
who could do
anymore black shoe.
The Colossus among us,
The Bell Jar too far.
That gargantuan body
of work in small
slim volcanic volumes.
Removed now from time and the personal
still sing in a unique voice. Quiet, commanding, savage and
strange.
Larking about. Oh yes. High Windows, a definite success.
Stevie in one or two. Cavafy I love.
But aside from Elizabeth Smart, gorgeous and drunk,
falling apart,
and maybe Tom, Tom the piper's son –
and I don't mean Thom Gunn –
Who?
Hart Crane? Yes.
Yes to his muscular despair and that new old world.
Still there isn't really anyone
who speaks to me as you still do.

A light. A night.
We're through.

How did we get to this place?

How did we get to this place?
Where Rome burns and we fiddle?
Where Caligula marries his horse
and we applaud?

Every despot loves confusion.
Feeds on fear and frenzy.

The poor are castigated forever and ever
berated, for daring to be.

Tower blocks overflow and burn
and even those most privileged know
that shame is now ashamed to sit.

The thermometer is up.
We're about to explode.

We who are about to die
of hunger, bad housing, neglect, do not salute you.
We despise you and deplore you.

Was that change ever really coming?
How have we allowed the years to roll back?
By being silent and brave and not vigilant enough.

Turn on each other and on ourselves, forever
imploding.

That's the history we are fed.
Hunted and haunted.
Exhausted and humiliated.

Running, running just to reach where we once were.

There wasn't just a plan to destroy us, put us back in our
kennels, keep us afraid.
There was an ideology.

A ban, a trap to stymie our success. Reverse our progress.

How did we get to this place?

Through forced smiles, acquiescence and greed and need.
We hope you like us, as we press our faces so hard against
the windowpane
we suffocate.

Too late, they whisper, too late.

Annihilate.

The Stain

There really is no alighting from the poverty train.
        The hooks sink that deep. They sink and
        sink to fathomless depths.

The subtle terror of poverty.

In a second, in a moment, at some function or
        opening. Or anything grand, embossed,
        golden. Even the invite suggests you've
        stopped being a small person in the big
        game. So fancy. Shiny. Yet you shrink like
        Alice and diminish at a word, in a TikTok.

That stamp. That stain on you. That fear of
        discovery, recognition.

Power is intoxicating. And being offered a seat
        at the table is so seductive. Just right.
        Correct. Earned. Why not sit?

Mingling with people where there's no connect.
        Have you no self-respect?
        Shout. Stand up. Walk Out. Why not
        object?
But those memories feel more real, that yesterday
        more present than this sunnier, airier, leaner
        life now.

These droplets reside forever inside. When we
            wrapped ourselves in blankets and cried from the
            cold. Heating cut off. When we couldn't pay the
            bills. They are before me ever. At the corner of my
            eye, at the centre of my vision. There. A blue flame.

We heated baked beans by candlelight. We almost starved. It
            felt romantic. Special. Their glossy red coating and
            smell revolt me still. I am haunted.

This Dr Jekyll and Sister Hyde, this arrogance, this
            everlasting hunger, this angry, anxious hybrid
            creation of a man, chiselled from and borne upon
            these moments and memory.

They help focus. Cradle fear. Conjure the meaning. Ever
            inside me.

He was so tired

He was so tired he couldn't move
when the ants began to eat him in the sun.

The sun ate him too
while he lay unresisting
yellow and grey
it ate clean through.

Like an opera, a symphony,
he sighed and ceased to be.

That silence, that stillness,
a boy unparalleled. A grenade of a boy.
On a frozen, sun-drenched day
floating, levitating, carried him away.

I wanted him to know

He put Parsifal on and told me to
shut up. *Parsifal! – Weile!*
It had a silver cover, the LP.
It was from Bayreuth, 1970.

He put his hand around my neck
and looked into my eyes.
'You silly little queer,' he said.
'You silly, stupid little queer.'

And I thought I might die.
He slapped my face so hard my
ears began to ring. *Kundry screaming! Kundry singing!*

I pushed him back and he ripped
my tee shirt downwards from the neck.
'This is what you like. This is what you want.'

He bent me double to my knees.

We met in a disco,
over 35 years ago.
I'd gone back to his because
he'd said Parsifal was his
favourite opera.

Mine too.

And the whole bus ride we talked
and laughed and flirted.
Diverted.

He pulled me to my feet.
'Say you wanted this. Say it. Say it.' *Kundry laughs.*
Is Klingsor pure?

With all my strength I shove him
away
and rip the record from the deck.
I hear it scratch. Loud and hard.

He looks at me, then at the record in silence.
'You scratched the record,' he said.
'I didn't want this. I've got to go,' I said.
'I was only joking. You shouldn't have taken me
seriously,' he said.

Silence. Silence. Luminous silence.

'I've got to go,' I said.

I even tried to joke. To joke.

To make him feel secure and make sure he'd let me
go.

I think about that warm night 35 years ago
and I wanted him to know.

I'm So Happy I Can't Stop Crying

She set the house to burn
then went to work.
It was that kind of day.

Her hands bled through her gloves.

Rivers of blood. No-one stared. No-one noticed.

She kept her hands in her pockets
all the way –
red wine stains around
her pocket and mouth.

She sucked her fingers dry trying
to drink back the blood
that had poured out.

She caught her reflection whilst shopping

turquoise, sublime,
blowsy and bulbous
flashy and afraid.

I'm so happy I can't stop crying,
she said.

Holding my breath

I dream, and I dream
that my life has
become a dream.

As it has.

The days slip, slide
glide away.

And the memories
on delicate, fragile
ice, drift towards me.

I see right through the ice.
It's lacy
and blue. Not
cerulean, like the
sky, the colour of eternity

but the pale liquid
frozen blue of sailors
who try to whisper something
you can't quite hear,
when you are dragged beneath the waves.

Beneath the foam. The sound

I am afraid of this
refrigerator blue. Of its
loneliness and despair.

And its grace in welcoming me in.

Jezebel's Daughter

In this gilded room here I sit.
Waiting for the change to come

Am I it?

Or does my gaze lock too readily on the man?
Then man to man to man

All Humanity.
Smiling supreme,
I flick my hair
And change one life for another

Just
Like
That

I change the red room
for the grey.

And artichoke (which I never knew
how to eat)
for peas and cherries.

I'm restless in the kitchen
and wordless in the bed
maybe I might
in the middle of the night,

but by day the idea is dead.

There is, you see,
no end to me.
Or my proclivity.

The thousands of miles
I've covered
and the millions yet to come

Lovers
divined combined

fragrant and rank,
vulnerable, invisible –
blank?
Stretch out before me,
their radiance like the sun.

And Jezebel's daughter has just begun.

Nora (for Kfir)

Stronger than death you are. Oh, Nora,
don't slam that door.
Don't shake the children from
their gossamer sleep.
They breathe so quietly, I think
they are dead.

Instead,
Nora, stay.

And speak.
How clever you've become.
Or were you always?
So clever to let me
glimpse that childlike side
and think it's you.

Was that your adieu?

So womanly, so brave. So fucking foolhardy.
Don't close that door.
I won't. The dogs will bite, leave big red
marks on me. They are untamed and
you set free.
The children will blame me,
until they grow old.

Nora, hold.

But pull that door shut quietly – so
quietly on our lives, on the home I
thought so large and dark and free.
Which was really only big enough for me.
As you tiptoe out to the void
vanish into a million little
pieces which we could never put together again.

Think of me and the children,
we are partners in your silent play.
We were your followers that you threw away.

A wall is a door
A door is a gateway.
A door is an opportunity.
A door is a cage.

A doorway to walk through
is also a doorway to close.

The Undead

Clearer and clearer calling to me.
Silver on the wind. Leaves that cut.
Breath on my windowpane
disappears then reappears
overwhelming the room
the fear you are not near
drives me insane.

Tap, tap, tapping
the scream of the vixen
the growl of a dog
all senses heightened.
I want you here.
We conjure you here
for our epilogue.

Sean. Stevie. Derek.

I hear you but cannot see you.
Like my dead cat, you prowl
and shimmer, light footed. Aware.
I hold open the door,
it vibrates with you. Right. There.
The rush. The silver snow in the air.

Stevie. Sean. Derek.

There in the pipes, there
in the wood, the concrete,

the lift up to the 12th floor
the doorbell, the hallway, through the kitchen,
the room shining and shimmering with view.

We may not know your stories
or your histories, or your songs, books, tears,
but we know them.

Derek. Sean. Stevie.

And now the room, and now
the street and now the earth
is full of you.
The absence throbs, finally full.
It's spilling over, giddily we
drown in it. Here. Here. Hear.

The dew on your eyelashes as big
as pearls on damp grass at dawn.

We won't be locked away, they say. Or held
at bay.

Like paint we mix.

As the thinnest line of reality melts,
our stories now inhabit the same room.

Know your names illuminate
the world

Derek. Stevie. Sean.

The Charnel House

Lit by lightning. The sodium
smells, a snake in a
circle, engorged and engorging its tail.

Lit by lightning. Lit by lightning.
The dirty toilets in the clubs,
the sniff sniff sniff. The sweat.
The view of the river, Old Father,
as I wandered, not sure where to go.
The electricity of possibility sang within.
And those arid nights where
I caught the night bus to go back home.
The dark and moody pub in Tooley Street, where we
met. That place
is the plague, the plague, I'd say.

So we moved to the East End.
Popular it was not. Your joke. But we
liked those big square white
rooms. Reckless. That prospect.
And the night-time journeys.
Sniff. Sniff. Sniff.
And the closeness, the speeding up of time.
The drugs. And the hazy drawing away. The
drugs. Desire
pushed us further.

Lit by lightning and blood.

I became very ill. Was I trying
to leave you then? I drifted
and hovered and
wasn't there when I was there.
But as long as you held me physically,
you didn't care.

I got worse and worse (maybe on purpose?) so
he'd have to let me go. But it pulled
him tighter. He squeezed and
squeezed until I wasn't
there at all.

The day of the eclipse, I looked
out over London, my love.
Grey, a shiny pearl grey beckoning
and I said, 'I have to
leave. Let's leave Poplar.'
But he didn't want to let go
of all he knew and start again.
'We can't afford to.'

I cannot stay, am afraid to die. But that coward
inside me could not give himself up.
Refuses to step outside the door.
He. Just. Won't. Leave.

The go looked like a green
light until you inspected it
closely.

– That wasn't the way it was: I can hear him
screaming, That's a lie. That isn't the fucking way
it was –

The club, the afterclub, the drugs,
the drink.
And this newer city with its falling
wall beckoned.
It would nourish us. It would
refresh us. We would wander its
East European streets endlessly.
We would, he said.

I slept 22 hours a day.
My illness a tapestry I pulled close around me for
warmth, a tattoo covering my skin.

I wouldn't answer the phone. You'd
call from England and I'd lie.
I ran and ran, yet kept crashing
into you.

Then I was sure I'd seen you in a café. Hallucinate
you on the Metro. I'd see you in all those
men I met. It's what I'd like in them –
the familiarity, almost being you.

But when I saw you I couldn't stand that
despair, and your resignation
to my dying, so long as I died
with you.

And in those streets, and in those
streets lit by lightning
I found my way again alone.

That's why you hated me so much.
I had discovered
a cure, found a way to be without you.
I couldn't say it for such a long
time, but when I did, you didn't
believe I could
be alone.
Find another
dream. Heal the huge hole I'd torn
in my life.

I wish there were a conceit
to cover this pain.
I wish there was a lie to
make us whole again.

I wish there was a time
that we could bind once more.
To laugh and walk and talk again,
as before, but refreshed.

Renewed again.

Were we so damaged that we
ruined each other's lives? Is that
why we met? To fulfil that
purpose for the other?

I think of you every time I am ill.
And those passions we conjured are with me still.

NIGHTINGALE

I understand, as I do not understand. So willingly I give my
heart.
Notes. Nocturnal notes hurled, thrust thrillingly into the
night.
I cannot bear the beauty, too lovely, it tears me apart.
Yet something about this disintegration of self is true,
is right.
Who are these dark archangels? My thrilling dark avengers,
their beating wings vibrate like hearts. I hear their keening.
Their sinister splendour.
Calling me. Calling we. They glare reflectively. They scorn
danger.
They rend their feathers, their claws, their beaks. They mark
my door.
Protect me in the blackest night. They hover, they flutter and
dwell.
Their lullaby sung so sweetly is all that gives me rest,
whose wings are shield and armour and protect my
fontanelle.
Help cure me of this melancholy. I am a man possessed.
Your certain protection makes me gasp for breath.
And the fear of fear itself holds a mirror up to death.

Roulette Russian

It was one of those old-fashioned train carriages that
smelled of sweet wood
with a large table to eat, read or play upon.
He didn't look up as I sat down, was
staring out at
South London speeding by. Slight, defined,
he touched my leg under the
table almost immediately.
I was in the corner by the
window. Raising his leg encouragingly against mine,
he still didn't look at me.
I cleared my throat.
His eyes
flicked up briefly. Cornflower
blue. Or maybe slightly
more violet. Yves Klein blue.
When he looked down
I could study him.
His face was all planes.
Smooth and untroubled.
He pressed my leg and I pressed
his. So ardently. With such
a promise – what delights the
sex would bring. My foot moved to his crotch.
and tapped there rhythmically.
Tapped to let him know how
good the sex would be, how
hard I would fuck him.

He got up to leave at the next stop.
He leaned over and whispered,
'I'll never forget you. I will never forget you.'

This was the Middle Ages before mobile phones, internet. Or
apps.

But sometimes, late at night, stumbling on my way to the
toilet I think of that boy.
Several ghosts in the hallway
run, hide or disappear, afraid when
they see me.

But he always waits, pale and
slim. Smiling.

Flowers that bloom tomorrow

she. hand outside
the window of the speeding car,
of the man she just met. leaving the handsom
fuck at the
end of the lane.
not sure what
he'd done wrong. so wrong.
down that copper lane.
she hated the countryside, but
loved the idyll.
the dream. the perfection and
completeness of the Violet evenings
and the lemonade with ice.
the normality.
the equilibrium. the placid calm.
how she craved all that.
and she saw the madness
and she saw the grief.
well-rounded and friendly.
soft to the touch.
and she said, 'for fucks sake
don't listen!'
it wasn't her song, but one she'd
learned.
and it wasn't her truth
or a portent of the frightening times ahead.
or that her horrific past was

not a thing to own. or hold. or claim.
but the grace was all her own.
and the song sang true and
clear, like sunlight on water,
like a quick dazzling thing.

shewolf. witch. earth mother.
goddess.

picking up another man at
the phone box.
'can you help?'
she said. what she really
meant was, can you stay?
can we discuss? fight. argue.
love?
her unbearable degree
of individuality.
that faultline. that savage cross
to bear. all her own brew.
no-one could have guessed
the flavour. or the taste it would leave.
'carry me on the wind,' she said.
'carry me. let me float and
fly.' almost invisible,
just glimpsed. a silver thing.
seen. seen.
what is it about those dangerous
days that start so well with

sunshine and laughter?
and beauty.
she dared state I am here.
and I make my stake.
i deserve to just be.
to take the long path, mess
up, fight and scream.
to be unapologetic. and ugly. and happy.
me.

Haunted Teeth

At eighty-five years old, she was gnarly, snag-toothed and
        bent,
and decided that false teeth were needed, to eat properly. For
        beauty. To be content.

Without her pearly whites in she found it easy to lie. Easy to
        cry, to flatter and to soothe,
but once she put her false teeth in, they clattered out the
        truth.

The bitter truth about her, her friends, her love, slights and
        wasted time,
but once those gnashers snapped in place, she couldn't care
        less about saving face,
and the sarcasm dripped like honey from her lips, surprising
        and sublime.

She'd never made an enemy before the saga of her teeth,
yet when those savage choppers started, it felt like a relief!
Her early life was choked by mendacity and deceit.
As soon as she plopped her teeth in, she could not be
discreet.

She had smiled and smiled her life away. But anger distorted
        it to a scream.
'I've only ever been pleasant and nice, is this all a bad
        dream?'

Careful, crafty, she'd always bit her lip till it bled
and never made a fuss,
still once those teeth clicked in place friends named
   and shamed her a cuss!

So bright and lovely, so tombstone large, those fangs
   just couldn't shut up.
They snapped and snarled. She was Medea, she was
   Medusa, in a teacup.

They offended. They hurt. Made people fear her, run
   away.
'It's not me, it's my haunted teeth,' she'd say.

At 15 years old

At 15 years old, I was sick of waiting.
Waiting for change. Waiting to happen. Waiting to become.
In the limbo of my bedroom, contemplating
how I'd emerge? How I'd resist? If I'd succumb?

My life before that was shrouded in fear, doubt and shame.
I hated my walk and my voice. Too girlish, too slight, too
            strange.
Being seen marked me out as a target for blame.
I knew I must own who I was and change.

At 15 years old, I'd carry my school uniform when I would
            go clubbing
and went straight from the clubs to school.
I felt alive and dangerous, alien and cunning,
not afraid of breaking rules, of hostility or ridicule.

And I have never asked permission nor waited again.
For when to wait. Or go. Or remain.

About The Author

Robert Chevara is an interna-
tionally-acclaimed, award-
winning artist, writer and
director. His output spans the
fields of opera, film and
theatre, and his productions
include seminal works
by Shakespeare, Williams,
Ridley, Verdi, Bizet and
Adès. He has written several
opera libretti and contributed
to poetry collections, and is
equally active in the arenas of
political engagement and both
visual and performance art.
He divides his time between
London and Berlin.

Photograph by Francesca Bondy

Author's Acknowledgments

I was helped enormously with advice and revising my poetry
by Kfir Yefet, Lyndall Stein, Regina Nathan, my mother
Pamela Callaghan and my husband Jörn Horaczek. Thank
you to my brother Rikki Beadle-Blair for the wonderful,
heartfelt foreword and lastly to John Gordon whose care
helped birth this collection. I am deeply grateful to all.

Also available from Team Angelica Publishing

Prose

'Reasons to Live' by Rikki Beadle-Blair
'What I Learned Today' by Rikki Beadle-Blair
'Faggamuffin' by John R Gordon
'Colour Scheme' by John R Gordon
'Souljah' by John R Gordon
'Drapetomania' by John R Gordon
'Hark' by John R Gordon
'Fairytales for Lost Children' by Diriye Osman
'Cuentos Para Niños Perdidos' – Spanish language edition of
        'Fairytales', trans. Héctor F. Santiago
'Black & Gay in the UK' ed. John R Gordon & Rikki Beadle-Blair
'Sista! – an anthology' ed. Phyll Opoku-Gyimah, John R Gordon &
        Rikki Beadle-Blair
'More Than – the Person Behind the Label' ed. Gemma Van Praagh
'Tiny Pieces of Skull' by Roz Kaveney
'Fimí sílè̩ Forever' by Nnanna Ikpo
'Lives of Great Men' by Chike Frankie Edozien
'Lord of the Senses' by Vikram Kolmannskog

Playtexts

'Slap' by Alexis Gregory
'Custody' by Tom Wainwright
'#Hashtag Lightie' by Lynette Linton
'Summer in London' by Rikki Beadle-Blair
'I AM [NOT] KANYE WEST' by Natasha Brown

Poetry

'Charred' by Andreena Leeanne
'Saturn Returns' by Sonny Nwachukwu
'Selected Poems 2009-2021' by Roz Kaveney
'The Great Good Time' by Roz Kaveney